SOONER OR LATER FRANK

Jeremy Reed

SOONER OR LATER
FRANK

ENITHARMON PRESS

First published in 2014
by Enitharmon Press
10 Bury Place
London WC1A 2JL

www.enitharmon.co.uk

Distributed in the UK by
Central Books
99 Wallis Road
London E9 5LN

ISBN: 978-1-907587-41-2

Enitharmon Press gratefully acknowledges the financial support of
Arts Council England through Grants for the Arts.

British Library Cataloguing-in-Publication Data.
A catalogue record for this book is available
from the British Library.

Designed in Albertina by Libanus Press
and printed in England by
CPI Antony Rowe Ltd

CONTENTS

MONIKA, JUICE AND TOMATO SOUP

SOONER OR LATER FRANK

AFTERLIFE TEXT

NEVER TOO BUSY TO BE BEAUTIFUL

SMOKE AND MIRRORS

THIRD WORLD WAR BLUES

NOWHERE TO RUN

WHAT BECOMES OF THE BROKEN HEARTED

'You'd never know it buddy
I'm a kind of poet
And I got a lot of things to say'

Harold Arlen *One for My Baby*

———

*for John Robinson
and Mark Jackson
with love*

MONIKA, JUICE AND TOMATO SOUP

MONIKA, JUICE AND TOMATO SOUP

The zips are vertical on her black coat
four incidentals that I pull
into a fetish, a detail
like a jeans fly or waterfall,
the coat riding to ankle-length,
her black reflective glasses black on black

signalling implacable cool
her speciality's tomato soup
done Polish, 8 chopped tomatoes
the spiky onion roasted on slow flame,
the basil littering like seaweed rafts
across the Mars red surface: it's the X

factor goes in it makes it hers,
a tasty instinctual signature.
Her black hair's Cleopatra fringe seems blue
as thundery cobalt, and she's my juice
today for poetry – the image I
manipulate through my hot chemistry,

her coat the starting point, then her eyewear
lifted on irises so cornflower blue
they look like bits of floaty sky. Her name's
the way I think of her, three syllables
that seem like a flower opening to a voice,
her smile responsive to the energy

I juice at her in small persistent squirts
of weird adrenalin. Her black T-shirt's
cut out at back, a teardrop shape on skin
like a guitar and works into a belt
shot pink and silver like a galaxy
dusty with glitter, and she'll never know

that she's my model or read a poem
about tomato soup, or how she dips
a spoon to try the simmer, adds garlic,
and lets the taste settle, like her sexy,
optimal, brimming, one hand on her jeans
hiking them to a plateau on her hips.

WENLOCK ARMS

A summer there in sticky warehouse heat
our fuzzy light-polluted sweat-drenched thrust
to monetize a dead friend's books
boxed into dusty architectural blocks,
dealers categorizing firsts and states
Red Snapper partners itchy for hot cash
both of us maintaining dandified looks
in repurposed high-end Shoreditch,
it's rogue outtake the Wenlock Arms
looking like a Krays gang operation,
peeling green walls, purple frontage – I'd knock
at 10am for Aaron's flaky need
to stabilize, a drinks top-up
kicking the pineal with a sugared boot.
12 handpumps, a stripped-down defiant room
yeasty with real ale smells, I stepped into
a throwback parallel space-time
scrutinized for my beret and paste rings
crowding on starburst clusters at the bar,
an edgy glitter, a moody lagoon.
She never spoke, just handed me the glass
as dodgy hours breaking the law.
Two months, two hours a day deconstructing
solid book tons as physicals, we sold
into profit – I kept a CA shelf
of Robert Duncan like orange sunshine
stored in the pages, had a last drink there
like flipping back to 1958,
got all my times wrong, bussed back into town,
knowing I'd be too early or too late.

THROUGH THE BAR WINDOW AT THE MAGDALA

Right through the bar and out the big window's
light-travelled push on South End Green,
so many stars mixed in the galaxy
to get this, and a plane tree's shot down leaves
detaching in November, gold pigment
turned blotchy on frog-skin green,
and standing there I note Glenmorangie,
Bushmills, Jack Daniels, Famous Grouse,
Glenfiddich, Gordon's, Pimm's, a list
that's accidental mania,
space given to write on the wooden bar
in hacked-out purple Pentel on paper
like double helix bite, I get a word
leads directly to another
a line that's poetry, a signature
so individual beside a stain
that's London Pride, a circular mapping
I trace to John, he's on his eighth,
and for the moment the counter's empty
giving me a big sweep of things, the light
at 6pm that's like crushed strawberries
graduating to lavender, pre-dark
I look out at, noting dark blue
inclusions – and I get it done
that solo privilege, writing there upfront
before the gang arrive and fill the space
with reassuring talk, what's lost and won
in simple living, day by day,
the window turning dark now and our drinks
lifted directionally towards the sun.

BLUE STREET PAINT

That blue paint on the street, cyan-turquoise,
a pill coating Viagra blue
as postmodern text, cyberbattle fonts
or formulaic urban hieroglyphs
a diagrammatic Thames Water code
in peacock arrows an asymmetrical
tetrahedron signposting Coptic Street
South Hill Park Gardens, Peter Street,
a trio of sightings today
like street art randomized as lost and found
in spiky Sudoku boxes, cool grids
in Colgate Oxygen blue – pavement slash
like cryptic puzzles that I quiz for clues
to inner pathways, neural networking
that's fuzzy haze, like a fogged barrio
beside the tangy docks. Most London days
I arrive somewhere like it's invented
off-message to the Lonely Planet Guide,
an alley twist, a submerged court,
the complex geometry of a locale
I've never visited, but recognize
excerpted into my reality.
I'm blue-spotting today for chalk or paint
like the blue ribbon network, find my clues
where others miss out, posted in a yard,
on stop-tap covers, like mental haiku
left by street pirates on a concrete chart.

ST GILES BLUES

In Marlowe's parish – Kit the punk pirate
with Pete Doherty's bandit attitude
to lawless brokering of sex and poetry
hung out there, dodgily turning a trick
like pushing back the tide
with a single hand, green river water
dragging a booted rent boy down
at Southwark. Renzo Piano's Central St Giles site
projects orange and blue apartment blocks,
luxuriously bankable real estate
as high-end chic: you'd die in there
forgotten as a baked beans can
cupboarded and beyond its sell-by date,
that central, it's a floating ecosphere
with its own purchase on low smudgy cloud.
Some flowers in the churchyard, red begonias
like bleeding cherry pie don't make notice
except in scratching my physical memory
today, tomorrow, then they're gone
like all the things that I don't need to know.
A VMC Plant cleans the road –
a lumbering burnt-orange truck.
My afternoon's composed around these things
as urban blues, those little happenings
that sometimes mean I'm in or out of luck.

HONEY

A spoon's sufficient, viscous floral gold
bee-lifted by worker flower-probes
sugar-addicted buzzy fur
irate as Goodwood reverb
in bitty tumbling blossom,
ended on my blackened toast.
In Highgate once, I lay flat on my back
for Matthew's shoot, his tomb-robbers series
the nameless grave corroded
like a urinal, and there were bees
collecting somewhere with unstoppable
piloted energies, each sugar fix
like doing sex in a frilled corolla.
I roll my honey on to multi-seed
like expanding a sticky teardrop shape
into an asymmetrical island
for a sweet tooth getaway, a drenched crunch
to an accelerated 8am.
Matthew's dead of a pill-crammed overdose,
his photo book expected, and he's there
inside my honey jar each time I raid
its contents, and remember how he shot
me, arms extended, arranged on the ground,
bees droning close-up at my head,
and with each bite I recreate the sound.

MY LONDON

www.jeremyreed.co.uk
new books like *Piccadilly Bongo, Bona Vada,*
the digitized city, the urban physicals:
each time I write I fire-up two million million
myosin molecules – my Pentel sign pen
7275 like purple carbon rocket casing:
the London smell like opening a gherkin jar,
sniffy, micro-bacterial,
the city floating in a tidal pool
sulky as a blue-grey submerged opal.
Nachos Mexicana or Spinach Lasagne
for lunch, or Mezze with Baba Ganoush,
think toxin-reactive vegan.
London's so many off-message modules
I'm always off-centre imagining a door
accesses the lost capital
tagged by a red Chinese graffiti slash.
My re-modified heroes with uploaded genes
live in that space and never lose the look.
I use No7 Protect & Perfect Intense
50ml anti-invasive light pollution,
a lick of firm-up collagen from Boots.
Most journeys take me back to Newport Place
WC2 as a basis: choose a basement bar
to perform poetry – I'm on a star
aka the Ginger Light, we squeeze the place
to saturation, beats our signature.
My busy streetwise eye pulls quizzy video
all day in detail-obsessed grabs: meet me
down on a wharf facing the river's groove
its green direction dictates poetry
the way it flows, and maybe we'll be friends
sweetening the moment like sugar in tea.

SPREAD BETTING

It's like spread betting what I do with words
impacting car-chase imagery
into blue-chip investment poetry.
Alan socks away shares in Drug Giants,
Pfiser's blue diamond, and he takes it too,
Viagra's rocket-booster energy

on rainy Sundays, pops the bubble pack
for the polymer-coated time-release.
I manage my portfolio of lines
back to a wall writing outside to track
the city's Soho clued-up energies,
no money in my empty writing hand,

my DNA strips coded on the page
as work inked to a blue smudgy tattoo.
Once I worked at the Dilly, pulled a man
out of the crowd, my looks sold every time
to feed a habit – fuzzy poetry,
the risk addictive, like the dopamine

flooding my brain on the station's concourse
or up above on the explosive street,
twenty minutes, my head starting to spin,
I mean somehow a poet's got to eat.
I'd do it all again, collect the light's
slow dazzle, ripped over the Haymarket

to a slashed strawberry-purple sunset,
subvert the state to get a line come right.
Alan bets on megas – Glaxo Smith Kline,
Johnson & Johnson, it's his voodoo lounge,
and tends a deep burgundy cyclamen
the way he does a friend with little cares

accumulating to a shared index
of stabilizing trust. It's one with me
to give my poetry like blood, sit out
soaking up West End atmosphere all day,
compressing bits I see into a mood,
the things I do and still they never pay.

DEATH DATE CUTIE

The spoon stands sentry by the strawberry jam
a compressed fruit Waitrose cheapie.
I probe a chunk like using a helicopter
to peg the washing line, a chunky cone
shaped like a sugared Mars moon.
My death can't be outsourced, it's done solo,
and not branded to sell or be hijacked
by a predictive text fuck duck.
What if I had my own expiry date
date-stamped invisibly on my hand-back
as a gene-coded real time reminder
I've gotta go, one autumn day
with fog bushing the white chrysanthemums
and planes grounded in the damp air,
no Gaultier Classique jacket
breathed on my shoulders. The time's never right
like jam volume in a donut,
but it's precise like a white robot arm
attaching a storeroom module
to the science-labbed International Space Station
slung together as a bashed docking-point.
I've got my moment when the error's due
as a blackout – like the dark side of the moon
as tipping point – I'll love you to the end:
today the hail cracks in like tumbling dice.

BITTER BLUE

Ten years of benzos, bitter blue UFOs
Valium the colour of air miles blue sky
flipped from a 10mg blister pack
to deregulate my anxiety
or nail file crumbled to dusty granules
I'd palm-lick at rush-hour, stalled on hot track

back of the carriage, panicked in the crunch
of dumb commuters crawling between stops
in depressed surges on the Northern Line.
I fed a phobic habit, stockpiled drugs
like neural weaponry, dose-sensitive
to GABA uptake – I could feel the drops

like air pocket bumps in my chemistry
and worked to get the edgy level right,
that desperate I rubbed it on my hands.
It turned against me, I broke up at times
on a weird signal when the drug misfired
its coded messaging like a handgun

exploded into my personality.
I wrecked relationships like furniture
with missing arms and legs, but wrote all day
through some integrated autonomy,
got two doctors, then three, and hoarded pills
and never spoke of my dependency

to anyone, prescription drugs big-time
that damp emotions and reverse effects,
my blue comforters turned perverse on me
and messed me up, as though programmed to feed
on my confusion – I'd lose it in crowds,
shoplift, and meet blanks in my memory.

I got off slowly, replaced tens with fives,
went down to twos, and drank, but found a space
clear as a Boeing's window on blue sky
and had it colour up with rainbow bands,
but still it comes back most days how I rode
the Central Line – a poet with blue hands.

STARBUCKS PITCH

Most iPad entrepreneurs broker there
informally, this cool-look dude
in blue cuffed Levi's, zippered aviator skin
with a fleece collar like a chilled-out csar
sips Caffe Americano
and plots like he's watching a tennis game
in which the ball bounces before
it hits the court, a wave-like quantum freak.
It's the new global conference space
a floating island with teal-blue armchairs
and street windows out on to tomorrow
that's just more colour faded than today
like sun-bleached jeans.
                      I go there most to write
and people-spot: South End Road or St Martin's Lane
for tobacco-brown faux leather sofas
and the scooped insulation they provide
against big-city rush. Blueberry muffins
have mushroom-shaped summits that look like clouds
stacking to a cobalt ruffled Frisbee,
the lemon drizzle cake's like summer snaps
taken in sun-drenched Hawaii.
I write my Starbucks storyline, modern
cyber-stylist facing a mustard wall
one tone yellower than Coleman's,
a novel that absorbs the end of time
as a banal crash – bankers on the run
into the desert, and looking out now
I note after low cloud a dusty orange sun.

PERSIAN RED

Your ten Persian red fingernails
are shaped like mini table tennis bats,
neon red, shift a continent
they're China red, and fixate me,
like your pick at lemon polenta cake
molecularly.
My ID's poet, as a snapshot stamp
or for chemical iridology.
It's so outside what you'd expect,
it's like sitting on a deserted beach,
in hyperactive Waterloo,
I'm daily pushed to an edgier edge
an off-world slice of accelerated time.
I guessed your finger polish matched your toes,
I'm glam obsessed, and as lateral shift
wonder if Morrissey ate a cheese sandwich
in real time as I'm writing this –
a poem adapts alternative lives,
multiple personalities?
I bring your red nails back into focus
as a fetish, vermilion
or scarlet detail, in the red index
of talking to you between memories.

EVERYWHERE'S NOWHERE (BOB DYLAN AT 70)

The years accumulate as left behinds
like city signposting viewed from a car,
the outlet malls, rainy red LED displays,
one gig replaced by another's
whiteout amnesia, the moon-faced white
polymer coating on a sleeping pill,

it goes that way, a lost moment's
100 years ago – it's Tallahassee,
Alabama, New York, London O2,
always the full on explosive present
littering like a contrail – shotgun songs
shattered with vocal bullet-holes,

the scorch-marks burning fingers, snapping strings,
the road extends his life five thousand times,
his air-miles shimmy in global carbon,
the body narrated into the pull
of lyric gravity – you hear it too
an edgy spiked-up 'Like A Rolling Stone'

or desperate 'Tangled Up In Blue',
the songs familiar now as oxygen;
the car burns on through foggy Birmingham,
Nashville – a biker on the road
doing a crazy segue – and he's gone
sloganing B&B – Bush and Blair

Criminal Blood Brothers, a red sun up,
an uncapped bottle of Jack Daniel's
targeting raw spots – there's so much to learn
from whiskey's altered state intelligence
under a jet-rumbling eruptive urban dawn
like a popped tomato, moving on again

into the hills – and it's a Dylan day,
the exchange of place crucial to the art
of moving songs round like playing mahjong,
blues at their heart, lifted out of the land
as tribal rhythm – and he picks it up,
the pieces quickly filled in by the band.

HART CRANE'S JUMP

The *SS Orizaba* – white on black
corroded ship's paint: dead on noon
April 27 1932:
Hart's in his cabin, drunk on Cutty Sark,
a sailor's cap raked on his head,
butch, bruised and beaten – it went wrong
the way it does inside a song,
the hurt compressed into a blues
muddy as mixing paint over a drain.
His pull's downward into a sky
that opens up inside the sea,
the centre of his deathbound hallucinated
gravity, the drop
into white water shattering
like an exploded window.
                              Somewhere else
in Cleveland Ohio
his mother shuts a window on the rain
and worries, and she doesn't know
what panics an accelerated flash
of Hart staring at her full on
as though he's back home and demanding cash
for drink and sailors.

He gets to the stern in a dressing gown
and vaults the railing, shivers there,
the momentum so powerful in his mind
it launches his trajectory
into the churning thrashed-out wake,
his skin still bronzed from Mexico.

His mother punches at a blister pack
of Aspirin for a headache scrunching nerves.
Hart's shipped in transit for New York.
It rains in Cleveland Ohio.
She doesn't really want him back.

GOING UP

The bottom's like a bad shoe-fit
that bites
2cm small, too tight
for the admission of full-windowed light
atomizing a burnt-out star
as gold shimmer on the floor.

I lay there once like tea inside a tin
the dark like tannins
in my veins. When I got out
I twisted honey on a spoon
like digging into sunlight stored
as sticky orange matter in a jar.

I made it up, testing the floor,
ground level, and a shape-shifting
blue morning glory shot with pink
chased sunlight up a stringy vine.
I steadied, did mood-adjustments,
tried not to drink.

The way up tested dodgy stairs,
a stranger's look made it for me
her smile from out a shop window
like a strawberry.
I met her later in the street
and mixed our chemistries into a date

for which she wore red shoes.
I tried and got above my loss
by small adjustments day by day
learning that way
the power of small things, like good pop
patterning the air-waves with sunny hooks.

Once up, I learnt to check my falls
like honey sticking to the jar's
slippery convex walls,
began each day with a gold lick
of bee-info, so many fields
spread on my toast like Provence in full flower.

BLUE HYDRANGEAS

They stump up like blue broccoli –
wavelength 440–490 mm
Prussian blue, ultramarine and cobalt,
rainy no-colour sky, pigment blue
and satisfy
with crumbly brimming reticence
a sort of garden apple pie
if it was bitty blue.
I go to them like seas I've never visited –
the Black Sea, Red Sea, Gulf of Mexico,
the China Sea, places I tell myself
are saturated navy blue
or lapis lazuli,
Blue light bends easier than red
in scattering. Sometimes a candy pink
gets involved like a complementary sock
a detail the eye fastens to.
Most days I leave them out of what I do
like a lover recessed backbrain
who comes through sometimes on a rainy day
when neither were expected.
Blue. Blue. Blue.
3 metres from my black back door
they have their clumpy bushy space
while I sing pop songs to myself
in holed purple socks sung for You. You. You.

PIE AND MASH

It's East End folklore, river food,
the basics liquored in a parsley squish
green as a Shad Thames tidal pool,
a pesto green the incentive
to float a crusty minced beef pie
in impasto emerald, like a ship's hull.
Colin goes Exmouth Market way
to Clarke's, in a black-trimmed, chalk-stripe crombie,
as a Krays throwback, 50s' gangster's fix,
and tells me the brothers dusted
with Max Factor before a job;
he knows and ate the dish with them at Bow,
after a sting, in driving rain.
It's his Saturday heist, breaking the crust,
his grey eyes slippery as seafood,
his voice so full of song, it takes the river's tone
at some turn of the bend.

He's energy
for one fixation, won't let go
the sauce's trail, it worries on his tongue,
the texture, dockside tang, it's never twice the same,
but almost, foots over to Clerkenwell
one fist clenched, like he's still holding a gun.

SOONER OR LATER FRANK

SOONER OR LATER FRANK

You end up listening to his quotient
     of rainy day, blue-mooded songs,
Sinatra sounding like he's in a bar
     by drizzly New York docks, the voice
a lived-in confidential baritone
     that always seems familiar,
bourbon-shot, 2am reminiscent,
     resigned, resistant to the hurt
he phrases neutrally, for bashed about
     means changing partners like a shirt,
a red-and-white striped Brooks Brothers affair,
     the tie dropped like a hanging man,
the attitude an emotional outlaw
     who never gets the answers right
and talks them into blue and indigo
     inflections, gangsterish felt hat
angled defiantly, tipped north or south
     for studio or for mafia wear,
and always integral to the Frank look
     that's in the voice: he's right in life,
so centred in it, he's like a peach stone
     pivotal to brimming texture,
but at the same time sitting in alone
     on loneliness, an Alka Seltzer glass
fizzing to opalescence in the hand,
     the woman gone, her Chanel scent
left as a fuzzy hangover. It's loss
     he builds on and converts to gain,
but still it's trouble, win or lose, and both
     feed into song – the ones you hear –
his pick-up fuming, just a casual bit,
     her lipstick bleeding on a coffee cup,
downtown, while he sits sorting out his socks
     to the soundtrack of steady New York rain.

4pm. November, the West End sky
blue topaz shot with jade and red
dispersals into indigo,
and someone in the shop whose energies
collected into a sonic figure,
light as a Gibson Les Paul guitar neck,

145 lbs fluency
of clean DNA – like a river's source,
hair like silver brushstroke calligraphy,
black leather jacket like moleskin,
a man lit with a diamond's clarity,
an oriental closure to his eyes

tracking the book shelves, and sighting the best –
Turkish White, Mind Fuckers, Chemical Ecstasy –
drugs as a psychoactive gateway to
an altered state identity,
like speeding up a downstroke guitar riff
to paradigmatic angularity –

'Stairway to Heaven', as the ultimate
troubleshooting fretwork, a violin bow
coaxing an edgier response
to sounds heard in the centre of the sky,
his ear a helix in the galaxy
soaking up space-time signals, star-chatter

in spooky wah-wah frequencies.
We talk of Yardbirds and spiked LSD
and Pentel sign pens – I hold the barrel
for definition like a guitar neck,
and have him share ink with a signature
patterned into a purple V,

pack up his books, while he forgets his pin,
cancels three times before he gets it right,
like me dyspraxic, and goes out to light,
a pink rip slashed over St Martin's Lane,
like cerise silk, the sounds mapped in his blood
coming up later with the sizzling thunder rain.

AMY WINEHOUSE'S BLUES

I like the chocolate voice genealogy –
Billie, Nina and Amy's piggyback
bluesy black gritty inflexions
phrased so generically down
they're underground, like cutting black diamonds
that sparkle in delivery

like lights on the Camden canal
shivering like a rayed-out tambourine.
Amy's Mill Hill Mississippi Delta,
her epic wacky 'Back to Black'
commissioning of a band's energies
into a graduated hook

comes up burnt orange – a pop glow
beamed light a sunny high that drops
back to a ratty narrative,
the conflict between pipe and blow,
the hurting, cheating, losing game
slashed across a woman's heart

like blood-graffiti, slogans burnt
into a shattered tag.
She shapes a song fluent as oxygen,
a crack diva got so skinny
she's like a curvy poppy stem in jeans,
and sexy like the vocal's symmetry

that's so inimitably street
it brings the grainy dirt alive
like stardust, as she lifts it right
into a molten honey fluency
of black gold, and the undertow
is like a subterranean river

an R&B Fleet or Effie,
her command like she's lived a thousand years
in 27, all that mad
desperation focused into her loss
that comes up shine, I mean her radiance
making the top notes sound so bluely sad.

ELVIS NEVER DIED

It wasn't Tupelo in Tennessee,
Memphis, Nevada or Katoum,
but in the sudden rip of raspberry light
a smoothie pink over Shaftesbury Avenue
I had this Elvis moment, a time reversal
seeing this teeny copy, the black quiff
deconstructed as moody attitude,
6ft, 160lbs, a pink Nudie shirt
slashed open under a black check dog-tooth jacket,
blue skinny jeans pegged into pointed boots,
the E-clone slipped into Nightmare Planet,
no fangirls in shock-waved pursuit,
no conflict signals noised by anyone,
taxis locked into a tailback's aggro,
big city pressure surfing in the blood,
and every random possibility
in the E puzzle a potential bit
to a London sighting, the light mixing
cerise and lipstick-red like poetry
over High Holborn's fuzzy pollution,
two mini-skirted retro Japanese
emerging from the store and me waiting
improbably, expectantly outside
to meet the petulant optimal cool
diamond showy snake-hipped rock 'n roll king.

LITTLE QUEENIE

A single pink nose-diving hydrangea
tumbles like crumbled macaroon
into a back steps cracked-up urn.
November blues – play them again
'Go Little Queenie, go, go go'
chased like a diamond star halo
into what comes up Saturday, like lists
I need to do, like American Dry Cleaners,
and Boots for vitamins and Panadol,
Waitrose for leggy purple sprouting broccoli,
Oddbins for all that black sunlight in wine
like bottled galaxies, and do
white baguette at Euphorium Bakery.
The big events happen on smartphone apps
even 220 miles above blue earth
at the modular International Space Station
slung together like white Leggo pretzels
travelling at 17,500 mph.
I alternate my errands with rewards,
things I buy to disperse the dragging blues
like Big Purple Quality Street,
the light continuing downbeat tempo
no-colour gray – I've got it on my phone
'Go Little Queenie, go, go go.'

AFTERLIFE TEXTS

EXTRATERRESTRIAL OUTLAWS

It's parked up empty on the Texarkana road –
a 1954 pink-and-white Cadillac,
colour of a strawberry ice cream cone,
a virtual remake or a car
resistant to degradable meltdown
waiting for the right Elvis to retrieve
its worked-out customized ergonomics.
We're carbon creatures fired-up with glucose,
the others, they're re-modified
extraterrestrial outlaws,
the come-backs written into history
who never got away, but still click on
to their updated legacies –
Burroughs in Kansas firing shotguns at noon
somewhere in woods St Lawrence way,
a leaky trail of blood and no body
marking the bullet-peppered killing field.
He still shows up on virtual methadone,
grey felt hat raked over reptilian eyes,
circa The Wild Boys. They zone in and out
space-times like aircraft rescheduled
on time-delay, flying out of the past
into the present, and their look persists
as optimal, iconic, hijacking
the present with image voodoo, sightings
arresting attention, that's Elvis runs
out of the rainy dark towards his car
as though pursued by girl fans in their heels
running to rip the shirt clean off a star.

DORIAN GRAY: THE PHYSICALS

Bevelled grey boards, ten butterfly designs
stamped in gilt, Ward, Locke & Co 1891:
an orange neon sun
120 years on
comes up, we're eating cinnamon and rice ice cream
from Lazio on Wells Street,
dilapidated pagoda turrets:
and the spoon jumps – 250 numbered copies
on Van Gelder handmade paper
signed by Wilde (for Dorian):
you know the future-forward jump again
zoning to dot and rib spiral condoms
for come-index and later pak choi
that tastes of tomorrow sealed in a jar.
Title page, half-title by Charles Ricketts,
three-quarter vellum gilt –
Wilde gave his copies out to Dilly rent
who sold on, what you do you do
and it don't alter, like this line I write
as a commitment, and Wilde never said
if Dorian's eyes were green or grey or blue.

MATTHEW LEWIS

Your soft voice brimmed like Manuka honey,
the active ingredient kindness
25+: I'd live inside that tone
like a bee piloting intelligence
into a flower, the shocking pink peony
open in the garden the day you died

as a ruffled explosion into frills.
You always sat on floors visiting me
like you were doing yoga over tea,
your shyness glittering your nut-brown eyes
with quizzical expression, you threw looks
that became photos, all those one-to-one

preparations before you'd shoot
the portrait, like you'd found the person out
as someone they'd forgotten, or submerged
in layers of defence. I see you still,
younger, gunning a black Raleigh push-bike
over to mine, and you were always late

from indecision or dull methadone
recovering with sticky chocolate cake.
We did a shoot in Highgate cemetery,
me lying on a grave, rose in my teeth,
and I remember the clouds moving left
as one-way traffic, and your reversed peak

and white T-shirt sloganed with attitude.
Later, you told me you were seeing things,
hallucinated stuff that terrified,
psychotic visions rolling in like trucks.
You disappeared, a drug-coshed casualty,
went missing to your friends. We saw you back

an altered Matthew and I never knew
the pathology that you'd locked into
as an invasive black parabola
attached to your brain like a jellyfish;
you never spoke the half of it, your pain
there, like the cherry stones left in a dish.

Your end was lonely, there was no-one there
to make the difference: pills mixed with sweat
before you swallowed and drink did the rest
on a showery bank holiday, the air
loaded with toxic juju. You were kind
beyond exception, and your work the best

in upping character, getting pop hooks
in facial expression, I'll miss your smile,
bright as an orange, and your quiet way
of giving everything to those you chose
selectively, and now the peony
shattered by rain litters a ruby spill.

FLIP-SIDE

Under the street again at Cecil Court,
a West End basement, repurposed cellar,
a lamp projected on the paint whiteout,
a book-stacked disordered bunker
I squat on a lipstick-red Chesterfield
a sort of Al Capone boardroom update,
a slinky retro-chic sofa
the colour of a slippery maroon leaf,
(it's October): you're counting out fifties
laundered in Soho, girlie-pink
crisp paper energies with enough edge
to slice a finger.
                              You cut ten grand
chopping units symmetrically
into thousands: a grand fills a wallet,
no ostentatious overspill,
your irises like blue oysters
that sort of cloudy marine luxury,
your lawlessness cut like your chalk-stripe suit
the perfect, slangy-lining fit –
I catch a flash of hot cerise satin.
Your look swims in and out of me
like driving on a rainy road.
I humour you, I know you've got a gun,
and bring you down to basics with strong tea,
accept your gift – fifty twenties
uncertain if I'll ever dare present
cool paper dodgy as my racing heart.

RED UMBRELLA

Tomato-red, a projected planet
150cm diameter
a mini-Mars – I'd found it in a hotel bar
a compacted vermilion sun
with a pistol grip chestnut handle,

it became my portable studio,
my cover on a thunder-showery beach,
the circular desert island
I'd maintain writing teeny poetry
in saturated blue moods, toxic blues

like sweet poison at seventeen.
All day I'd cloud-spot for blueberry mousse
impacted cumulus like a mauve brain
staring down the beach like a white runway
and I'd squat territory before the rain

with jet-whine tuning in the sky
and everything so amplified I heard
my brain-waves messaging, my blood
negotiating arteries, the storm
building its muscle over Brittany,

my loneliness compounded into edgy wait,
a girl in a hot orange bikini
standing up, towelling off, eyes posted wide
at the horizon, and the emptying
of the beach final, just me and my stick

waiting to project a red parachute
and seal my insularity
into a bubble, and I'd write like that
lit up by the slashing sizzle of rain,
the dry world reduced to 30 inches,

and hope it never stopped, and still today
I tent in rain under the sheets,
or walk the city with a red saucer
tilted at downpour, working poetry
out of a small space that's a comfort zone.

THINKING OF LATE BOWIE

The suited David Jones gone puffy now
from medication (it's Atenonal),
no persona put out for hire
the accent indigenous south Brixton
untoasted now by hot cigarette smoke,
the flat vowels level as the street
oikish with atonal cockney.
He stares out on Lafayette Street
Nolita and Notto's lofted bankers,
buzz-cut lawyers playing scratchy guitar,
the dudes who wash their hands in liquid gold,
dollars stuffed into burger buns,
a red sun facing down his retro shades,
like a planet dancing on obsidian.
What's missing's subjectivity,
there's no-one in the songs, no personal admissions,
they're empty as growing stressed plants in space
on a service module, their clues cut up
and scrambled into bitty accidents.
Bowie's late shape's like a Viagra pill
a blue coated modern diamond
that does a nitric oxide surge
into spontaneous disconnect, a hard
that's really anyone's.
Death's not an option, a slow boat to China's
not available, he's left to face it out,
the present, like a conical grey cloud
the colour of the building it crosses
tracking its slow shuffling way across the river.

IT'S THAT TIME OF THE YEAR AGAIN BILL

The only voice, Bill Franks' and his flowers,
bitter evergreens, white chrysanthemums
that smell of compact China tea
and purple-throated stargazers
and a burnt-orange stung with beauty spots
lily, and roses the colour
of cool urban-romantic poetry,
the sort I write (so does John Ashbery),
and it's December with JetGlo Express white skies,
an aviation high gloss paint
that matches the season, like my
Japanese white spider chrysanthemums
stiff as a shirt from the cleaners
spiking the arrangement: it's Bill's again,
this poem that I'm writing on an arc
from Newport Place to grey tidal Vauxhall,
the river coming up a muddy green
as fluent moving backdrop in my mind
and tracking with weightless poetry,
it's just a sequence, a global computation
of brain rhythms that come up right,
a unilateral thing – I can't get back
the neural input that I give,
but Bill's a part of what he'll never read,
his flowers giving a pine scent
to things I do at home, things that I live,
and always more demanding what I need.

PISSING INTO THE BARBICAN LAKE WITH JAMIE MCLEOD

The lake's a black tower-blocked
obsidian slash
deep as the London underground
a lit-up urban hologram
like a UFO looking in
on toxic shivery freeze.
We chill outside, pre-interval,
waiting for Marc Almond to bleed Jacques Brel
into a shattered torch ruby –
'The Devil OK', 'Le Diable Sa Va',
done like a shocking urinalysis
of lyric spiked with wild
English garlic. We won't go down
sub-podium to the deodorant cubes
submerged in urine, but whip out our cocks
for a steamy duo on the pier,
our yellow pigment urochrome
and mine fluorescent from B vitamins
and Jamie's clear, his nitrogen
the hissy deposit.
They fill in now, three triangular towers –
Cromwell, Shakespeare and Lauderdale,
and we describe glittering arcs,
a sort of subversive piss graffiti
into the pond – and seven floors above
under a white barrel-vaulted ceiling
I catch a boy doing karaoke
liberated into subtext, arms thrown,
while we in midstream make the water ring.

CRIMINAL LOVERS

The dark's like thunder downstairs at First Out,
a blue spot angled on the mike
at which I'll read fisting ruby sequins
and hot pink glitter surges in the air
a poet making pop of poetry
a dynamic demanding style, a look
that kills for attitude, Jamie McLeod's photos
and trashy slashed graffiti texts
called Criminal Lovers on show,
dark, desperate dandies of the underworld,
top hats, piercings, bruise-blue tattoos,
a gangster suit striped like a rainy day,
they face out on two floors, these London lives
fixed into concentration on themselves
as preparatory chemistry
to Jamie's shoot. We work the energy
before the singer does an impromptu
moody shaping of 'Criminal Lover',
Marc Almond dressed in a black coat
doing a slow-burn knife-twisting vocal
to fix the room. We separate
into a black St Giles December night,
go taxi-spotting in the city's rush,
each feeling the criminal in ourselves
up for review in the edgy street light.

REMEMBER ME

The look's always a slouched beret,
the hurry real – I like a street
that dodges into an alley
Fareham Street to Diadem Court Soho
a cross over like one space-time
connecting to a different parallel
and in the court a purple door
(it's there today) like a pop hook
buried in change, and a viburnum snowballing
white rayed-out flowers into scent.
A London moment's worth a year
in optimal experience, I've lived
a thousand at burn-out intensity
like a Ferrari's scorched tyre tread.
I map familiar alleys where I can
an alley-cat networker across town
like fitting my arteries into the city's
in fluent motion narrowing
to a back yard and London's uncrowned king –
a gangster in a charcoal chalk-stripe suit
rapping in a busted chair, black hair gelled,
doing an urban bongo blues.
I'm here and there and one day gone
into a dead end, but today
hurry through Ingazeby Court to Garrick Street
clear of the passage into orange sun.

NEVER TOO BUSY TO BE BEAUTIFUL

MOMENTS

The tricky insight when I find you out
I mean the nearest I can get to know
you in the corner of my eye
green as a pea
turned upwards, doing yoga with a thought,
a flexy 3D diagram
you're imaging, neural networks
firing from the brain's 100 billion neurons
(there's 400 billion stars in the galaxy)
isolating a little twist that's you
like grooves in a green pasta twirl
or a poem in an anthology
condensing something to a condom fit
it's that close to retrieved experience.
Once looking out the black window at night
I saw a flash of sunlight hit
The International Space Station, a sprawl
of silver modules transmitting a signal
from off-Earth to my eye by chance.
The radiated moment
had me spontaneously dance
for singled out attention, and today
your look travels that far in mental space
I only guess it when you reconnect
the thought you had like shaping a diamond
copied in angles of your heart-shaped face.

RED PEONY SOLO

A solitary compacted ruby fist
explodes solo, showy hairdo
doing mid-summer hoodoo
out back where I scrape a rickety chair
on oxidised nosebleed supports

into coercion with my sit,
a pre-dark chill, my neighbour's barbecue
smelling of burnt sinew and fat
as its damped toxic residue.
Cloud traffic moves left, all of it

single lane, mid-speed alto-cirrus.
I refocus our cerise peony,
size zero stem like Amy Winehouse shot
locally in skinny jeans,
her head too big for a body

cellularly reconstructed by crack.
My Russian neighbours paint their kitchen white
inside and out, pill-coating white,
their language letting English go
sounds like a Moscow chat show,

temperatures soaring against cool
rollered application of paint
the colour of a Polo mint.
Her blonde hair twists like a gold bar
lifted from a protective cloth,

I see it ray-out platinum,
he's down low, like a spider, out of sight.
The flower's information lives in me
molecularly, I've a gene
coded with this extravagant peony,

and sit with it, as night comes on
like a face in the crowd I'll never know,
the one seen from a moving bus,
eye contact made; the flower my last look
bolting the door against the edgy dark.

RUSSIAN TEA

A black tea in a black tin from Moscow,
note perfect for the lemon drizzle cake,
black as a city's underbelly,
streaming, tangy and matte black
as your eyeliner's looped contrails,
your look maxxed up with blue windowed air miles
processed through cloud architecture,
and my brain a three-pounder universe
networking words and sexy geometry
as shapes I throw from the hippocampus
that's weird as Russian acrylic
I can't read printed on the tin.
I've 10,000 different types of neuron
coded in my system: the afternoon's
so cloudy it's like an éclair
split open on the fill. And your green shoes
bring cool mint to mind, regenerative green
like resistant hyacinth shoots,
all the associations dusted into tea,
and Russia abstract as the moon
to me, like China and the mustard Yangtze,
and you'll hold on to what we've got tonight
thin as a silver trail of pure telepathy.

RED LIPSTICK

At Yauatcha instantly identifiable
as a Mac Russian red bullet
a hot-tempo vampishly glam
vermilion, a red
like filling a white bath with strawberries

for big scarlet volume
and done triangularly, lipstick art
gloss-sealed like coating on a pill
as her doll-faced Tokyo signature,
silver mineral glitter dusting her eyes

like photoshop.
Her partner looks a Ponzi scam
a fraudster breaking paper trails
a Bond-type with a bullion truck,
I do thriller plots sighting men

who drive a gun-grey Bugatti
and shoot their plastic like a gun.
I flip to visualizing maroon sedum
turned raspberry coral in its outtakes plot
at home this sticky September, a spray's

like spiking China in a glass
the land mass shrunk
to a damped pimply garden flower.
There's so much compression in the moment,
such lucked up light-speed imagery

I planet-hop watching these two
and their sensitivity barrier,
she's sex, he's moneyed access to

the city as a marble dining-room.
Her red petulantly themed lip geometry's

 full on, and her mind's anywhere,
but sometimes clicks on me, then disconnects
in forward-drive and I fixate
on how she's focus for a stormy red
pitched into grooved lyrical symmetry.

RAINBOW COUNTRY

Jersey deposit in a plastic bag –
a mini-beach, black bladderwrack, scrunched grit,
volcanic, quartz glitzy, a winkle shell
that's nipple coloured, bitty, chipped,
an iridescent oyster lid
all scooped and knotted in a Sainsbury's bag

by Christiane to give me back my origins,
I've dumped on a mauve-painted kitchen shelf
between a perky Coleman's Mustard jar
and Fortnum's Sir Nigel's Orange Marmalade
and left there to get a rotting beach smell,
a tangy compost on a meltdown star –

the London I inhabit, meaty czars
and terrorists; and crunches if I squeeze
the contents, nip the orange carrier's ribs,
a crab's claw in there, olive-green pincer,
and eye-socketed cracked nacreous shell,
a mixed-up mortuary bagged at Grosnez –

the beach shelving into ripping green sea
fuelled like it's a stop-off plane. My coast,
the one skyscrapered with eyebrow rainbows
dissolving my teens into a purple glow
still swims molecularly into my blood,
the light prismatic, seven-band, shimmery,

smudged like a girl's thundery eye-shadow,
dispersed sunlight scattering through raindrops,
the red light highest, the blue innermost,
they came on like a marine Las Vegas,
red, orange, yellow, green and indigo
after a shower laid over St Malo

fuzzed into sunburst as a sign I kept
of sometime dazzle, someday poetry,
and get back prodding sweaty green seaweed
lumped in a carrier to know the high
of rainbow country, all that diffused light
doing hallucinations in the sky.

A LIFE IN FRIDAYS

The Friday rain's like fizzing gin –
the carbonated sparkle flooding base
in a plastic airline glass
at 30,000 rocky feet.
Magnolias the purple of sea urchins
impact and litter in Tavistock Square
as explosively sensual entropy.
Your husband broke you like a Lego chair
the glossy white nuts-and-bolts kind
upstairs in the Photographers' Gallery
on Ramilles Street where I write
to let window space in my poetry
like light in a blue diamond.
We talk of burnt-in pain that won't repair
like car paintwork that mends itself
when exposed to sunlight. Your photo mags
and sticky chocolate cake for chemicals
don't do the trick for emotional climb-out.
You talk round hurt in your Japanese way
of mini-bites, your mouth a red loveheart
twisted to angles when you phrase a loss
as a personal finality.
Friday's in the filling, a rainy one
like a lifetime's brilliant moments
dispersed as inconsequential dazzle
over Soho, brightening the memory
of what we share, your past as the present
scented by shampoo traces in your hair.

SMOKE AND MIRRORS

SU'S TOP FLOOR

The skylight floor shows planets like smarties
a bright space-dust cosmological mix,
a yellow, blue, orange river of stars,
their fine-tuned frequencies feeding
by signals her astrology,
the charts she maps because we're all stardust
with big rocks in our chemistry
molecularized into DNA.
Her black dress over jeans is a Yuki
a Top Shop snatch – her loop of beads
aqua Indian glass chasing navy blue.
Her world's compression, big to small:
if the sun was shrunk to a microdot
the earth would orbit
just a few centimetres away
I introduce as a sci-fi concept
to what we do up there on the top floor,
her cushions coloured like cassis cakes,
her eyes converting star glitter into
another hot connective energy.
There's a piano submerged by ginger plants,
photos of dead Tony, a mat
picked up in Ankara and big gold stars
on the ceiling, the way all the world's books
make up a thousand billion kilobytes,
she compresses the planets into types,
the city night building up as white noise,
and an abruptly banged cat flap
alerting us to a ball of striped fur
sprung up the stairs with eyes like traffic lights.

SPLEEN

remixed from Charles Baudelaire

I'm like the king of the rain country
grown prematurely old and camp
the damp eating my gold fillings
I sit up all night by my lamp
I'm toxic like a syphilitic thing.

I'm like the king of the rain country
bored with his hounds and scored with apathy
I don't care if the human race
dies in front of my balcony.
My jewels are lesions pitted in my face.

I'm like the king of the rain country
even my hired roué can't sing
a song the colour of my poison ring.
I'm bored as a coffin with my harem
their make-up doesn't mean a thing.

I'm like the king of the rain country
slouched on a couch with opium
like a trippy Chinaman:
not even thugs who manufacture gold
can save my blood from turning cold.

I'm like the king of the rain country
the Roman blood-baths, faggy boys
kept as the emperor's private toys
don't bring me half-alive, I live
as though I'm buried in my grave.

I'm like the king of the rain country
grown prematurely old and camp
the damp eating my gold fillings
I sit up all night by my lamp
I'm toxic like a syphilitic thing.

SMARTIES

A sugar-coated planetary mix
a compact Rowntree galaxy
8 colours never coaxed out in one spill,
but accidental in the palm,
a random free-fall, an orange,

a nipple brown, carnation pink,
like a new sequencing of traffic lights.
The red stain like a sugared wound,
the bright blue's a special event,
a Viagra blue, a new century blue,

a chocolate centred optimistic blue,
the one that seems to come up luck
demoting green and violet
to subordinate choices,
the art's to massage one not two

for the distinctive top and bottom notes,
the orange is a happy pill
a sunny planet in the hand
working for the saliva hook
like a garage band.

The green's evasive, elusive,
a salad or poisonous frog green
and needs to turn a trick with brown
to bump up personality,
its gloss coating appears sly

or tinted with glazed jealousy.
The art's in throwing smarty shapes
I close my eyes and rattle out
a shake of three or four
like edgy dice hits in my palm

and never turn up four the same
for luck or whatever it brings,
trying an accidental pour
for quirky sequencing, the melt
like a sticky rainbow smudged by body heat.

CLOSER

Death's like the shark's fin in the bay
accelerating out of haze
to hang in closer on a scent.
Each day the wall walks in
fractionally flatter
to my chest, no give at all
an ordinary blue-grey
painted wall
turned into an edgy minder
reading my blood-pressure, heart-rate,
cholesterol, urinalysis.
Paranoia turns a wall into intelligence.
At night
I stare at a red traffic light
instead of the imaginary future
I accessed once moon-walking into sleep
slow like an encounter
with weak gravity.
Even my blood circulates faster now
at Formula One speed
day by day towards blow-out,
blackout, whatever.
It's all that much closer
like internal
weather, stormy motion moving in
exciting in its drive
bringing me face up
to the resistant need to live.

MY DEATH SHIRT

A friend's sumptuous legacy –
I keep it hanging under polythene
a customized John Pearse purple velvet
red-stitched affair, a thunder-cloud
with sleeves and blackcurrant lining

measured for Martyn with his cells
piloted by viral kamikaze,
he had six months to live, frothy April
piling on burnt magnolias in the yard
like shattered confection, his life in bits

and wanted out and drew his shirt
as configurative reward in bed
to soak hospital visits in colour
so saturated it blanked illness out
by density, each blood test a frontline

report on cellular war, T-cells down,
the virus nearing the blood-barrier,
his shirt's resistant personality
protecting him from diagnostic scares,
its full-on Meard Street stitchy pedigree

so irrefutably supporting him
it became Martyn when he couldn't be,
the splash associated with his look,
a sort of cranberry-coloured substitute
for punched out dynamic, the accomplice

to dying in a way he could control
propped up on pillows wearing at the end
this blood-hot fetish for the final shot

dispersing pain, and given me
by his sister weeks later as postscript

to Martyn's ashes – a gritty sachet
sealed from his meltdown, and hung up by me
in storage to await my time
if I can wear it as a purple splash
in the last countdown facing a lights out.

THE DROP

Five, six tomorrow violet-blue
punchy nose-coned grape hyacinths
twisty as a mascara brush
do April redos on their site
some dark blue as a blue suede shoe

in Memphis 1956
and pointy like asparagus spears
re-territorialize their patch
skewed on their stems like cocktail straws
spiked into granulated ice.

The sky's a Boeing studio
a sonic mix of 737 drone
as aural London radio
no let-up in volume control,
the soundtrack in my head all day

like engine charts
dominated by whine. Most times
I hope it's a black stingray-shaped UFO
I'll locate sighting through low cloud
a disc compacted by intelligence

based on a star, an alien thing
like a turtle in the sky.
I click on UFO files instead
for encounters with accelerated
objects, and there's a diamond drop

of altered physics bending time?
My blue flowers angle a crane's arm
towards gravity, like those

notching the London skyline up
as diagrammatic concrete

into the cyan-drizzled air.
I stay indoors and Toyoko
finishes gunning her wet hair,
lets go the dryer and rays out
inner sunshine like a rainbow.

JOAN TIERNEY GONE

50 a day
ubiquitous Marlboro Lites
choreographing Chinese characters
in loopy calligraphy
the way smoke writes the user's poetry,

your fag quotient scorching bronchia,
your three sons, streetwise, born to lose
and running wild, rock and hash in their veins.
I was your unadopted child
writing my poems back to a brick wall

spearheaded by purple buddleia
notching up saturated scent
a sticky orange ooze to butterflies.
Terence first broke through the death barrier
in Thailand, trying to overtake the light

and impacting with thunder in a tree,
his bike exploding into flame
at 27. You grew deep from that
like playing mahjong with a praying mantis.
Martin went later, a rare brain tumour

brought him to London to see me;
you held his hand and felt his pulse blip out
to join the dusty galaxy.
Kevin and I remain, our emails fired
across the universe like superstrings

of blue telepathy.
He's one lung down, my nerves got shot
writing my weird side into poetry

as explosively neural imagery.
We both hang in on what we've got

owing so much to you, what's great and small
in being individual.
Two's not a number, better three.
One will go first, follow you Joan
out through the exit like a car tunnel.

RED LILIES

Cracked open like the ring-tab
on a can of Coke
without the sans-serif logo
8 Nova Red
Coca Cola red
showy extravagant tricks

erupt in steamy cloud-smudged June
as rayed-out propositions in our yard's
tumbledown greenery, self-seeded strays
doing their thing like me
aberrantly,
no basis for our stay

as transient facts, theirs two weeks
and mine precariously day by day
in a disruptive century.
They're here like botanical
extraterrestrials, red starts
to breakfast when I sit a while

with them for mismatched company
like being with a silent date
awkwardly outside a café.
I dig into honeyed muesli
for nutrient quotient.
My day's no bigger than the small event

of poetry, the signs I write
to which they're indifferent
like most people, except the mad.
They're bunched round like a local gang
hanging out on a corner spot
not knowing why the place attracts

as local, popular
and keeps on pulling by its gravity
until it seems the only place
for attitude, like my preferred
back of the house sun-up breakfast precinct
raffish with lilies in a rundown space.

CHÂTEAU DU PARADIS

Our red pour for a week at 6pm
a Saint Emilion Grand Cru
this bottle No 033570
the cork a blackcurrant nose-cone
the wine like tilting thunder in a glass
a stormy ionised crimson
blackout that puts us into symmetry,
a lateral shift in chilling out –
I'm here a week and gone a year
and noted with you an ecosystem
damaged by the Shell-sloganed docks
an energy from waste incinerator
polluting light. The water oiled dark green
with industry, we parked and looked out flat
across the bay's deep lapis lazuli,
the moody Jersey harbours 5pm.
Back home we did our evening thing,
the bottles lifted from the kitchen floor
full of their meditative storm, 5 years
of yogic habituation
in the cool.
The first glass takes up issue with the third,
the second misses out we find
on altering the chemistry,
the gain in altitude is gradual
to optimal – a bottle each – one more
and later we talk of its flinty origins
the grape's quiet simmer feeding on the sun's red roar.

RED CURRANT JAM

Today I think Eltham
uncapping red currant
jam in the planty kitchen
and visiting Barry MacSweeney there
(I'm re-reading his Odes)
hand-printed by Ted Cavanagh

on mustard-coloured paper
and how Barry was doing
tangy Moroccan black
his bilateral focus
all over the place
his joint packed as fat

as a sign pen barrel
glowering with altered state,
the soundtrack in the flat
Blood on the Saddle
Dylan's first stripped down leathery
'Tangled Up in Blue.'

We sat on a Persian rug
hallucinatory teardrop patterns
rubies bleeding into
turquoise DNA helices
and said only Americans
wrote poetry good as the drug

we shared for its sparky toxins.
Barry's dead from drink
the bottles he drank
could be stacked to a skyscraper
a glass London gherkin
and blew up his pan-sized liver.

Eltham's off my map
but Barry's poetry
mixes with red currant jam
that wins my taste today
the kitchen brimming with orange sunshine
that just might stay.

BUYING CUP CAKES

At 42 Tavistock Street.
a fuzzy drizzled diamond-grey Monday
an L-shaped diagram away
from Jubilee Market's tables of paste –
its exploded brooch galaxy,
I sight the shop painted like a lemon houseboat,
the Primrose Bakery, after three tries
of misdirected whiteout blanks,
(the street always goes missing or I do)
in Covent Garden's tricky mazy map
of streets constructed like a Lego swastika,
and it's my destination, cup cake days
for Toyoko, time out from a two-day affair
with Robert Duncan's poetry,
I'm writing on orange sunshine in its chemistry,
a CA orange as photonic mix
in his spatially visualized lyric,
and debate pastel icing tops,
and choose a lavender speckled with cobalt
and a chocolate dusted with turquoise stars
as confectionary artefacts
I have to manage upright in a box,
navigate back to Chalk Farm without jolts
to decorated cake nipples, secure
white cardboard mini-coffin in my hand
for Toyoko to break the seal
on sexy areolas, cute summits
sprinkled with star-belts, while the rain comes on
glossing the blotchy reds in grounded leaves.

SMOKE AND MIRRORS

My Mac studio fix writes in my face,
invisible foundation, what you see
is what you get predictably,
but off-image, I mean in the window
of Sherry's Ganton Street, you too dissolve
like a vodka squirt in a frosted glass
or blue light scattered in the atmosphere
its wavelength 440–490nm
cyan molecules zooming from the sun,
and yet you're like light inside a diamond
that's brilliantly optimally broken
into dispersal. Ganton Street's
repertoire of illusions shimmer today
like scintillating scotomas,
zigzag aura arcs, and outside the pub
the person I thought sitting out
was someone else, our eye contact
repeated intrusively, curiously
to no effect, his black reflective shades
videoing reflections, and when he spoke
his voice was like a brushstroke of silver paint,
his look a series of angles
a tricky unforgettable anthology.
Back home we thought of things we didn't buy
instead of purchases, our usual way
of doing things, like watching a contrail
cooling to crystal vapour in the sky.

FEBRUARY

I stockpile bottles against the big freeze
throwing snow shapes at the window,
air that has crystallized like a contrail
compacted to a white rainbow
and brought the sky down solid, powdery
into the street. I kicked through flaky sky

like a shattered windscreen getting home
with 3 Medoc as black tangy sunlight
bottled for back-brain reward.
My father's birthday 4 February
hurts in me – we were never right –
like atomizing paint against the wall

in random scary surges, I recall
the bad and miss the best
in him and mostly seem to disconnect.
If snow was purple I'd build a snowman
the colour of cassis, but it's so white
I cram aspirin to counteract

the rocky sense of balance loss I get
confronted by its sculpted tons.
The sky's dumped the weight of a jet
over our quarter, the dazzle
rayed out like a diamond set in London,
a blue rock that gets whiter as the night

comes down on my kitchen window.
A white arm outside on the scaffolding
is studded with brilliants and wind-pointed
with snout and tail like a crocodile.
I busy myself with Bordeaux jackets
grouping my bottles in their cupboard space

like clunky minders and consult my stars
Aquarius – a bad time for money –
lucky in love, release a cork
like a red-tipped bullet and look out
at flurried polka dots, and get a taste
of broody maroon uplifting poison.

THIRD WORLD WAR BLUES

THIRD WORLD WAR BLUES

We're back of Little Newport Street,
exact topology WC2N,
real time, already overtaken, 12.18
oppressive matte pink-grey with points of red
future-coloured skies, big rock space
the marker for no-oxygen species

revamped rehabilitated humans
injected to resist moon pathogens?
Our only weapon's imagination
that travels spontaneously fast as light
186,000 miles per second,
a mini-Big Bang when it comes up right.

What's there for measurement? Ebony's card,
a black Caribbean skin seen from behind,
her mobile given for assignations
like digits written up as state of art
apocalypse – she'll take you to a place
where consciousness turns into a love-heart.

The things at hand, they're jittery clutter,
Soviet badges, postcards, Chi Thai food,
Red Bull boosters: I look around a Jeep
blacked out ergonomics, an armoured fort,
sits in the traffic like Blair mafia
gunned into menace by a csar's minder.

What's in the moment? Two girls frame a kiss
like they're in bed, bleed pink and red lipstick
into a walnut shape and chase away.
A helicopter sights the Whitehall cell,
churning the air, its roters smashing through.
The Millbank bunker reeks of war jackals.

It's all in a day the war we're living through,
microbial fingernails, the urban shove,
the fat cats with cholesterol viscous blood,
the facts we never get a purchase on
like a blank office tower – and through it all
the light we still keep burning out of trust.

RED GUITAR: POP SONG

I want a kiss from a murderess
a lipstick killer blonde heiress
I want her Russian Red bullet
placing rubies on my throat
I wanna play a red guitar
in a Beijing bar like a glam rock star

It's World War 3 we're living through
Africa's full of Aids and flu
but I wanna play a red guitar
in a Beijing bar like a glam rock star

Bleed your lipstick onto my lips
over my nipples down to my hips
you're my girlfriend we don't need boys
they're using planes and tanks like toys
I wanna play a red guitar
in a Beijing bar like a glam rock star

It's World War 3 on the video
there's nowhere on the planet to go
but I wanna play a red guitar
in a Beijing bar like a glam rock star

Give me your love I'm tired of pain
kiss me again in the pouring rain
down by the docks and the China sea
wearing white socks like Morrissey
I wanna play a red guitar
in a Beijing bar like a glam rock star

All those czars who blow out our lights
let's take them on a tour of the sights
from Downing Street to Amsterdam
let's make them swim in strawberry jam
but I wanna play a red guitar
in a Beijing bar like a glam rock star

THE BIG GREEN TRIANGLE

A praline centre
in a green wrappered Bermuda Triangle
(a trapezium
of points – Florida, San Juan,
Puerto Rico) violet, peacock-blue,
but sometimes ink-jet emerald
like a Quality Street
Big Green Triangle
the one I buy for you
on sugar-itchy Saturdays
as a solid green artefact
packed with confected paste
like a Russian mafia's suitcase
shirt-crisp US dollars,
the taste
coated with impasto stick;
a green I associate
with neon or marzipan
or some kinds of opal
that look underwater.
It's the one, sometimes two –
a Big Purple as a pair
I'm conscious of as hand-luggage
cushioned in my pocket
as sugar-hits for you
who'll sit on them a day
like a plane gone off computer
before I find the foil wrapper
flattened rectangularly
into an admission
you've smoothed out the dilemma
with a pointy finger
as a cute afterthought.

MY NEIGHBOURHOOD

A loop at the top of a Hampstead hill,
I don't know anyone, they're like red shift
in quasars and hot star clusters
in the explosive universe
my uncontactable neighbours,
alien, white noise chasers, their 4X4s

blacked out, bullet-proof urban weaponry.
It's a place for widescreen big-city skies,
peacock or grey slashed by pomegranate,
carbon vermilions. I keep down low,
write in a basement like a terrorist –
the poet as a subversive outlaw

using imagination as a gun
to terrorize the totalitarian.
Some clouds show up – I give them names
as international drop-ins, sky candy
I'll never see again in the airways
and what would I do if a cloud came back

looking for me at edgy South Hill Park?
Some trees – a lime with heart-shaped leaves dusting
the street outside, it partners the night rain
instructively, lyrically at 4am,
when shaken out of sleep I'm fully up
confused and thrown out of my spotlit brain.

It's paranoia shuts down most contact,
defensive genes, I brush an eye sometimes
that sparkles diamond blue, resistant light
that lets me in so far, but won't attract.
Most flats are off-limits with blackout blinds,
the way in seems more remote than a star.

An orange dyslexic graffiti tag
spearheaded ROKIT points towards a yard.
I go to a gangster pub with a friend,
drink in the low-lit back room Ruth Ellis
did makeup redos in before shooting her man
six times, his body crashed on the road's bend.

PAINT IT BLACK

The valley loops like chi
spiralling into jump-started
beamed-up energy –
an armour-plated black-black Cherokee
glossy from spray colour mix
parked where your old fig-coloured Merc

oxidized under dripping trees.
6pm October cool pink slash
smudged carbon footprint in the sky
I'm back at your gate with a friend
stopping opportunistically by
the torched shell of your scorched mansion

an arsonist's reprisal
re-faced, repurposed on a site
hung over with bad aura
like dope smoked in a cellar
as a smudgy black rainbow,
the gates re-licked with paint,

video cameras sighting.
You so resisted death
I'm sure you only half got there
locked into a space-time
like a plane dipped off computer
and worried that your hair

would lose its platinum dye.
You lived on green bananas
and black opium paste,
Colombian coffee, kitkats,
nuts and had a taste
for chic and braided uniforms

and kept the house a ruin
gapped between dense chestnut trees
defaced by graffiti slogans
and a black swastika
for your Nazi sympathies.
Back there this inky drizzled day

I half expect you too
to show up in your black greatcoat
splashed by an orange scarf,
the new house with its lights on
backed into marshy badlands
like my twisted youth.

BAND OF OUTLAWS

One wore a bottle-green handmade Drakes tie
he'd nicked from Selfridges – I like that sort
who do panache without expense,
another read Thom Gunn's exercised cool,
and Seraphina the contortionist
pulled body shapes like sculpting chewing gum
to angles on a yogic stretch.
We'd meet at the Angel St Giles High Street
a dressed-down trendy room for banditry
the type that interests me, an edge
that won't be rounded, angularity
that's a lifestyle, but its ideas soft
like a praline-filled sensitivity.
Jake bagged me a poppy tartan Drakes scarf,
red, white and black check, a breezy mood board
lifted so the right person wore
the Liberty grab instead of money.
Nobody knew it, Colin's life inside
like being pulled out of reality
into a vacuum-sealed ID, a gun's
a quantum thing, you shoot before you think
and can't be in the two actions at once
and work through it for ten disruptive years
and later drink. We met there most weeks cool,
stripping our odd bits down to make them fit
a trust they're nearer right than wrong
in same company – it's always the way
learning the chorus first and then the song.

SAINT JOHN, JERSEY

A space-time, split-off, back of back
a no-time zone
I'd live in for its lack
of busyness, its sunken farms
(the kitchen light left on all day)
its landmarks, smoky blue hydrangeas
so blue they're lapis lazuli
bitty with washed-out denim blues
bushing a crunchy drive or yard,
my sightings all the way to Rue L'Enfer's
twisty tree corridor posted
in champagne gold 3pm October light,
a hot-pink rose like a Hollywood pout
making it late over the wall,
a mashed track looping off somewhere
in leafy density – 4,846 vergees
of parish secret as a snail's brain
and bumping up a steamy jungle green
teased out by rain. I'd live there if I could,
paint the interior purple, orange and blue,
and write at the kitchen table,
the sky on the back of my hand
as shimmer come off a blue scattering
of light, my broccoli punchy with anti-oxidants,
my tomatoes a sunrise/sunset red,
the day coming up slow, the big green day
lit by a slinky sea, the uncorked wine
switching on poetry inside my brain.

STEAL

Your first steal was like mine, compulsory,
the need to add a useless thing
a blue glass ring
to what you had, emotional deficit,
and didn't, a rhinestone on your finger
blue as an aqua swimming pool.
Mine was a trashy pulp-fiction thriller
Coffin for a Cutie, drawn to the name,
the jacket design, a Spike Morelli
juiced-up shoot-out sleazy thriller.
My impulse lost incentive, yours increased
to feed a habit, infiltrated chains,
you learnt to snip a tag out of a dress
deactivating security
and back home re-sew the tear,
your Top Shop rail expanding by the day
with things you did and didn't wear.
I found a different theft in poetry
and stole from people in their face
converting them to imagery
and put my words on show for people who
read as accomplices. We never stopped,
you couldn't fill the empty space in you
like a black hole, or me write anything
that satisfied, but as partners in crime
I wore your sparkly aqua ring
and you went out and stole my books for kicks
leaving gaps in my numbers on the shelves.

WANDERING (RIMBAUD REMIX)

I ran away a tearaway
a bovver boy in a torn coat
I ran away for poetry
in my ripped-up overcoat
a punk with a gold throat.

I tore my shirt and threw away my tie
the sky was full of crazy rhymes
I ran full on into my times
the stars were up there in the sky
I started plotting out my crimes.

I heard the stars burn overhead
on clear September nights, bright light
shone on me, I slept out at night
a runaway a tearaway
in ditches I got poems right.

I looked so down and out, the cops
sniffed at me sleeping in the square,
I drained dead bottles, I was through
with everyone, the words came out
my throat in colours, red and blue.

I wrote in a dark scary park
in bad places I knew my part
noodling my shredded shoe-laces
like strumming chords, my ripped-up boots
cracked like my schoolboy's broken heart.

STEPHEN ANDREWS

Sucked into a black hole, the disconnect
sugars my nerves like random noise,
white noise making London into
a 24/7
rocky recording studio,
and you're uncontactable Steve, off-world,

like playing Led Zeppelin's 'Stairway to Heaven'
backwards to hear the buried phrase
like a missing person
or neural Chinese whispers in the brain.
You're no longer trackable 6pm
networking alleys and courts in Soho,

clean of a burn-out coke habit,
still imaging the brain's reward,
a rushed uptake of dopamine
and searching for a substitute
in sex, AA and poetry.
I read you mine in a squeezed Bar Bruno,

you sent me yours like booster hits
of assurance you'd rubbed the streets
into your nerves like breaking laws.
I miss your dark green fizzy Saab
gunning me safe across town with the rain
sounding like irate molecules

brought to the boil in a saucepan
sluicing across glossed cellulose
on the Westway interzone.
You wrote copy for web pages,
wore a generic loner, an outlaw
to bonding, a trouble-shooter to ties,

but still it hurts to know you disappeared
without a word into the nameless dark
like a space probe leaving the atmosphere,
dead or alive I'll never know, my way's
to recreate you under raspberry skies
walking with me fast across St James's Park

the winter on us and the dark red slash
a fuming icy shut-down to the day,
the Mall like a white stucco wedding cake,
our hurry purposeful, our talk full on
as though we wouldn't come apart as friends
stopped for a moment by the moody lake.

GRAPE HYACINTHS

Ten make it up
like purple sweetcorns, knobby tusks,
blue graduating into mauve,
the colour's used lavender soap,
stems thin as lolly sticks
spiking depleted used-up soil

showery March atomized to rain,
the London I know collected
into my energies, a thrust
like NASA rocket fuel
lining my arteries,
clouds patterning like DNA

sequences over the city,
a survivor's toolkit
in my shoulder bag to fit
the edgy desperate times
I live through – the house opposite
blanked out by blackout blinds

a builder's pit
spaded back of it,
a shattered magnolia's D cups
showing cerise through ivory
the wind shivering its mass
like blackcurrant jelly.

Ten hyacinths can make a day
eventfully spectacular,
their resilience a figure
in survival vocabulary,
a stump of purple at my feet
communicating intelligence,

no matter ends are in the nerves
for our beat-up planet, the moon
an option for species rehab,
but for today, only today,
these beady mauve tops shine
like a collective star.

M&S SOCKS

Black cotton body, I like to walk black
underfoot, black at the ankle
like shirt cuffs, heel and toe
7 variants in this pack,
red, orange, blue, yellow, lavender, pink

and purple, horizontal stripes
branded under the colour block.
I like intelligent socks that think
ways forward like sci-fi lycra
tracking by sat nav and so cute

they're art worn flat like foot candies,
a hot pink with aqua contrast
or smoothie lavender surprise
like striptease back home on the boards
shoes left behind, the arena

for exhibitionistic socks
got into angled geometries
cross-legged or doing yoga
on a black-painted floor
rewritten into showy views

they never give in shoes.
Sometimes they look like stripy sweets
for toe sucking, the heels like orange hulls
on ships, a fit of metaphors
like Lego, sometimes they're like cats

with pointed nose leathers
and twitchy on a scent fidget
for contact with reality.

Mostly they bond with my Converse All Star
as black on black fugitives,

toe-puppets doing their own thing
in tropical colours 7/8
my foot size, and it's recreational
this giving them full play to be
two tropical fish detached from the shoal.

THE ROLLING STONES FIRST

No title, the mean David Bailey shot
speaks punk resistant streetwise attitude,
lit out of black, Jagger's right eye
in shadow, they're all left side on
like hoodlums bunching in a Soho yard
interrupted by spontaneous sunlight,

the Decca logo corner-boxed in white,
the undercover menace threatening
as London raw R&B hoi polloi,
they're image hipsters invading the charts
with deep south cooking, choked harmonica
sounding like a Jack the Ripper alley wail.

The UK length's 33-21,
16/4/64 release, that hard
it stayed 12 weeks as No. 1, each riff
lodged like a bullet in the brain.
The sound's lippy insurgent testosterone,
delinquent aristos throwing blues shapes

into rogue pop – it's all done from the hips,
the singer's pelvic elasticity
twisting a figure 8 out of his crotch.
They dress the music with cool style, sharp threads,
spear-pointed collars, dressed-down Ivy League,
black cab-black Anello & Davide boots

stacked up on heels. The Bailey shoot's that right
it digs the band out of formative dark,
as though they've reached another level there,
as diffidently visceral bandits
in edgy times – you see it in the hair
banged to the eyes and their indifferent stare

knowing they've nailed it, like 'Route 66',
a hustling surge of three compacted chords
ripping the song up like America
into their repertoire, and rush on through
muddy blues covers given sneering bite
that dips from sunny into flipside blue.

NOWHERE TO RUN

OFF-WORLD

I click on moonstates – dusty off-world
gritty acres of planetary blow-out
brokered for futures industry
3 days away from earth,
a shattered regolith, each impactor
biting the dirt like a mini-earth war,

the best investment methane propellant
manufactured for spacecraft resupply
without return to earth. I watch you dream
in cycles, making contact in your sleep
with bits of disconnected imagery,
as though in crossing space you're reluctant

to let go a resistant gravity
that pulls you back into yourself afraid
you told me later that your dead mother
was in the kitchen splashing gin
over an orange charity-shop dress
the price-tag hanging from it like a fish –

the detail weird as hallucination.
I'm a morning jump-starter, in the day
so fast, my speed is like a chemical,
while you delay involved in other worlds,
neural networks that you access alone,
a star wars game with a reality

that seems extraterrestrial.
I contemplate ten acres on the moon,
mineral rights, a land registration card,
a bit of rock swinging out in the blue,
a rehab-ranch for moon-based poetry
and mining Helium-3. You resurface

from REM, your black hair blown to bits
like standing on aircraft steps and your look
dispersed into confusion as you turn
towards me, green eyes breaking up and seem
a while in parallel realities
while I decide our next step in the universe

NASTURTIUMS

They tug up like crossed shoe-laces
a claret, violent orange-red
peppery diffusion
like a saucer-shaped UFO invasion
green leaves veined so incisively
unlike the human wrist highwayed
with violet knotty flyovers
they're precise like a tortoise shell
or open umbrella
studded with bright September rain.
I have to squat to meet with them
in deconstructed jeans, my height
throwing a shadow like partial eclipse
over their industry converting light
to pigment and nutrient
and ultimately entropy.
It's odd my getting down to London dirt,
tired, scratchy soil that's depleted,
but smells close up like memory
vacuum-sealed in formaldehyde
and of the grittier assault
of blood tasted on the tongue.
I do them sometimes in a salad bowl
for bitters or go stare them out
a flower-voyeur before dark
and dream of them beaming big orange light
into me like vitamin C,
and go back indoors with twenty red suns
brightening inside me like a galaxy.

MEETING PATTI SMITH

The little specs are professorial,
no ostentatious rock-star shades, blackout
defences, just the eye's twinkle
that turns on intellectual clarity;
the grungy clothes, navy blue coat, blue jeans,
black shirt, are instantly forgettable,
loose fitting, High Street store economy,
dumpy black leather bag muscled with books,
she's in her milieu now, gunning the shelves
at Red Snapper for Mohammed Mrabet's
Look & Move On, Anna Kavan's *A Bright Green Field*,
prose crackling with visionary sparkle
sharp as November frost's Swarovski filigree
calligraphy on a Russian forest path.
She sings along with Lenny Kaye,
without the tearjerker ache to Billy Fury's voice,
reworking 'A Thousand Stars in Your Eyes',
sweet, a capella, improvised octaves
girlier than her rock authority,
the softness touching in its clarity
the simplicity spontaneous for fun.
We talk, and sip bitter green tea
in Cecil Court, remember John Wieners
as one of poetry's luckless casualties,
burnt-out, burnt-up, resistant like his art
to a degrading visceral poverty.
Patti's here to record, her dynamic
less gutsy, rounded in its autumn years,
the way a leaf ripens from green to red,
the beauty always in the transition,
the brightest moment coming at the end,
the livid orange crumpling black, then dead.

YOU AIN'T GOING NOWHERE

A generation down or back
retro and blonde hair dye
won't re-track
what's missing, like I lost a car
in an amnesiac blackout
and recovered it in a dream
oxidized and redundant
carjacked debris.
A scratch on time? –
the fissures not apparent,
the swipe unit's deactivated,
the glass shatterproof.
A guitar rumbles power-chords:
the books I've read – slewed Panther paperbacks
are atomized inside my chemistry
like dark matter.
I'm disconnected now from source
like Médecins Sans Frontières
picking through radiated killing-fields
for impaced survivors.
I feel extraterrestrial
in Camden Town or anywhere
youth congregate: a throwback to
the rock archetype, Mod detail,
fitted jacket and patterned shirt,
dark shades, the undisputed look.
October reddens. Don't turn around
I tell myself: there's no return
to an idealized decade;
its glamorous shimmer adulated
by those who never lived it through,
but wear the present, turn its volume up
for colour, and today the sky
curves over, a bright cornflower blue.

PETER'S LAY OUT

One pink rose, snipped from the garden's jungled bush,
two litter petals, three or four
disrupt logistics in a room
mapped out by Peter's OCD,
he can't function if an object's displaced
3cm from its base
or if a tumbler's left beside the bed
belonging downstairs, it's an alien thing,
an extraterrestrial invading his space
beside the lamp and the Temazepam
rolled as white planets in the palm for sleep.
The blue house on Holland Park Avenue's
Peter's intelligence, a faded blue
No22
the numbers vaporized to faded haze.
Even a paperclip's like surplus weight
on a spacecraft, a book left out
or power on a warp or kink
in the system, a sensitive alarm
that's something out. I've been there so often
each second Friday, no fractional change
in placement, order, furniture,
the light trapped there as compressed microsphere
the colour of a green lemon.
Each room's a zone in Peter's brain,
the hippocampus, hypothalamus,
the limbic seat for piloting the ship.
A dropped crumb's like a golf ball, shoes removed
for risk of infecting the Persian rugs,
no give or take, Peter's bad foot
elevated on cushions, the traffic
drumming the double glazing like a fist.

MY END

I imagine a rainy Saturday
in September, nasturtiums pushily
splashing their pepper red, slash hot orange
UFO shapes in the back garden,
(I rent don't own) in a microcosmic
off-city blue chip NW3 –

the flat like Francis Bacon's at Reece Mews,
a workspace junked for creativity
into an unconverted floor
written up in personalized graffiti
as what I call my poetry
to which I'm addicted like Class A drugs

and write with the immediacy
of oxygen. I've thought of committing
to water, the solid black Hampstead ponds
at 3am, but it's a cold exit
hallucinating in a vacuum-sealed
opaque space-time, a dysfunctional fish

left to be dragged out by patrolling police.
It's private rituals, comforters I need
like books and music before cramming pills
into an infallible end
listening to Dave Davies' 'Death of a Clown' –
the poppy soundtrack that I'll take with me

into terminal shutdown, made up too,
like the song's draggy subject, cracked makeup,
and a last bottle of Château David
giving a basis to the pull
clean out of gravity – the bedside lamp
left on, like a white conical planet

against the final dark I fear,
some photos and John Ashbery books on the bed,
as last connections, maybe a red rose
as a punch-drunk signal, a floppy crown,
noticed a last time as indifferent
before the final ten million steps down.

MAROON DAHLIAS

It's the crimson full-fist size Bordeaux
red hairdos, spiky with white streaks
pull me into their seminal
October earthiness, the smell
of saturated rain after it's gone.
I catch their cool ray-out at Seven Dials,
reds, purples, brimming in a zinc bucket
like a crimson blobby planet.
I know Titan's layered in purple slush
methane-fat red and orange clouds building
twenty kilometres high
and somehow integrate this icy moon
into a metaphor for dahlias,
stems constricted by string like a rope trick
in bondage, karada
a Japanese submissive aesthetic.
Gem wraps. She's reading *From Russia With Love* –
Bond on his flight to Istanbul
drinking two ouzos, two Americanos,
two dry martinis, half a bottle of claret,
(a dahlia colour) – 16 units –
and partial to a vintage Bollinger.
My bunch seems such a maladjusted thing
to carry, a damp squeeze
I angle sensitively side and front
and sometimes bury, all those downturned reds
like redcurrant jelly in the jar's base.

TRAVELLING LIGHT

Thoughts of my end – it's right amygdala
goes into overdrive
signalling I wanna live
like I'm on a workout treadmill
in a compressed industrial gym

I once saw George Michael sweat there
a raw tang like geranium.
The apprehension's quantum
like attraction to potential
before a car hits the wall.

Today the sunlight's zillions
of local lime-green photons
drench St Martin's Lane Hotel
(I'm in the Starbucks opposite)
using it for reflective focus

like a smoked aqua light-box.
The doorman wears a black knit wool hat
for cool informality
and a velvet-trimmed charcoal greatcoat.
He looks like he was in a nineties band

that zoomed off-radar.
The girl left of me's bronze ankle tattoo's
like papaya ringspot virus
type – W, a rusty pretzel
with a liquorice all sort eye.

Most hotel check-ins arrive light
like divorcing information
from its physical vehicle.

We grow stripped down like the hipster doorman
mastering St Martin's.

I burn up time as poetry
the crunch comes with what I see
between it and what I'm writing
like a doorman in a Russian hat
who in the nineties used to sing.

WHAT BECOMES OF THE BROKEN HEARTED

44 BEDFORD COURT MANSIONS

for Alan Detweiler

Red brick façade: depress 44 for alert
no name on the annunciator strip,
unpolarized white noise: the voice come up
clear as Evian, like a teen idol
post-modernised – the future in its tone –

it always got to me like a pop hook
reflective earthshine in its molecules.
I'd bring my vulnerability inside
like brain-chatter, right into the kitchen
as the flat's modular brain: one to one

our meetings – jasmine tea and picky nuts
and weirding things to our reality
like SETI reading altered radio.
You went for numbers night-time Hampstead Heath,
the dark randomizing your faceless pick

in swarming woodlands and brought it back home
into your art: I have a white shirt still
given me off your back immediate,
pewter rivets on the pockets, a snip,
sometimes I wear it for creative thrill.

You compressed Lower Lodge into a flat,
your piano as focus, all those snapshots
of rent and street toughs scattered into spills
anthologizing dodgy attitude
you patronized as druggy juveniles

in local Soho like a Pantone figure
a sort of retro 80s' glitzy grey.
I'm at a loss each time your voice comes back
that you're compacted ash, the friend I knew
vacuumed, atomized in an ovened flash.

What I remember's the flat door open
already for a friend, casuals, bare feet,
the way I found you liberated into
optimal euphoria like brainfood,
and always present, there's only one time

to live in now – you maximized each day
obsessively, nicked avocados, pears
from Sainsbury's – you did it for the rush –
the kindness in you natural as honey
you gave away, Manuka 18-plus

active ingredient. You tracked downstairs
each time I left, keeping up parallel
on the blue carpet: how to make it new
this life we can't let go – I'd turn and wave
hurrying off down leafy Bedford Avenue.

MAURICE

December's hot pink ruffle in mauve skies,
you'd not have seen cerise at the hospice
on incremental morphine, tubed, alert,
the hurt in you sedated – what was it
still burnt in as irrational regret,
for terminal means letting it all go

your name Maurice, and your glitzy mobile
07801553289
now turned off: you the hot pink gossip leak
to underground networks, you made it shine
the bar you personalized, your smoky drawl
an urban cowboy brokering camp speak,

you on your sequinned cushion at the bar,
the style-avatar, and I see you still
gesturing confidential undertones,
batting your hand, a solo survivor,
your diamante brooch a glam paste star
the look so invincibly a cool kill

you threw performing shapes just sitting there
watching arrivals: gin in easy reach
a fizzed-up quintuple Bombay Sapphire
refreshed with squirts of tonic: you could teach
the drink intelligence, give liquid brain
to frosted tumblers pushed to overreach.

Your kindness got to me: you gave me scents
Tom Ford's *Black Orchid* and *White Patchouli*
and were just by your presence sympathy
to soft emotions, collecting outlaws
for healing tips: you got me up when down:
your attitude was an academy.

You've gone, the way we all do through pathways
we never navigate until we die.
You're there before me: the pink Soho sky
inviting your black woollen hat – so go
before you're old's the best thing – I look up
into this cold amazing raspberry glow.

MAURICE

Some people are exo-biography, by which I mean they so fully occupy your present space that they appear to have disowned their past, like astronauts on a one-way mission to Mars, without a reusable rocket to facilitate a return to earth.

If you don't know about it, you won't take the stairs down to the basement on Phoenix Street, located off Charing Cross Road into the subterranean Phoenix Artists Club, the inimitably camp Maurice Huggett's customized low-lit locale, the blue, red, green and white light fixtures drizzling angles on a room constantly revamped by Maurice's fussy relationship with furniture in the semi-dark.

I knew Maurice for fifteen years without ever attaching a surname to his full-on optimal focus on altering reality to its exaggerated camp equivalent. Maurice could shape-shift a phrase into hot pink mutable referents, give words if you visualize them zingy lemon-slice shapes, pretzel twists, potato crisp crackles, a lexicon of elasticated vowels, and a wicked twist of bitchy humour hissy with spiky venom.

Nobody ever really got into Maurice, because of the mirrored reflective surface of his personality. What bounced back at you, rather like talking to somebody gated by mirrored aviators, was those aspects of yourself you found in him re-modified. Not cold, like Lou Reed's sunglassed cool, but Maurice temperature, in which intimately confided gossip and sympathetic rapport were filtered through a middle distance range, like somebody looking at their own thoughts rather than fully at you.

Maurice

that low-growling, leathery, 50-a-day voice, baritone as William Burroughs' pitch; grainy, husky, the larynx scorched by hot smoke, they don't come vocally again quite like that, one-off tone, each phrase performed by habituation to camp. Accompanied by a gestural vocabulary of hand-bats, there was the one-to-one hissy confidential, delivered on the gold sequinned cushion on his bar

stool, so exclusive it was like being locked into French-kissing, the
declarative arc taking in the bar, followed by a 2cm readjustment
of his glasses or the impromptu delivery of show-tunes drenched
in the aspiration to spotlit glam.

Maurice

drank bottles, rather than glasses of Bombay Sapphire or
Gordon's: no measures, just immeasurable squirts as managed
update of a glass in which tonic was simply an afterthought and
ice and slice an obligatory citric tang. There wasn't any counting
of numbers, or apparent effects, other than a settling to a reality
made more comfortable by drink. Maurice swam into gin as a
stabilizing rather than destabilizing kick. It was like scuba diving
with his brain into a clear fizzing glass.

Every Wednesday evening the band of outlaws have our
academy there: a group of us meet under the street and talk
disaffection for mainstream culture and its associated politics:
rock, pop, nutrition, what's around on the street, the ups and
crashes in our individual lives, and of course Maurice who died
on 17 December 2011 after a stroke accelerated by his chronic
dependencies – cigs and a steadily escalating booze consumption.

Maurice

dead, is an extended subject of speculation: he lived in Burleigh
Mansions, a flat slung above Cecil Court connecting Charing Cross
Road to St Martin's Lane, a West End recess where for three years
I colourfully fronted the counterculture bookshop Red Snapper,
the centre of gravity for intransigent bohemians, Soho drug
dealers, indie rock stars, artboys and artgirls, all pulled there by
a fascination with collectable first editions and the fact I wrote
poetry at the desk all day. Maurice would appear in the shop
occasionally, looking like a molecular hologram in daylight, so
radically displaced I thought it was a virtual Maurice, to bring me
gifts of popular Tom Ford scents, *Black Orchid* and *White Patchouli*
that he knew were prioritized accessories on my scent-radar. It
was in and out: no book polarisation, his singular preoccupation
the Phoenix and managing a basement that was originally used as

a rehearsal and dressing room for the Phoenix Theatre, and never lost its sense of slap and stage.

Maurice

collected personalities, but not pretensions: neural sparkle, not money-sniffers, off-message not social networkers, sensitive and sensitized, not hedge funders. There was no television and a strict door policy to exclude rogue entries.

Maurice

most of what I knew about him was intuitively observed or got through enthused asides in which a tendency to self-mythologize was a dominant, like using saturated colour on facts altered to suit the listener. A flamboyant centrepiece to a room in which darkness was sliced through to reach the bar, each gesture from Maurice was a self-regarding signal, a camp semiotics like writing air-poetry. And to me as a poet, camp and poetry are inseparable: the elevation of the ordinary into heightened language through crunching sensory experience into imagery is camp in the context of achieving the line. Maurice threw poems, I write them: the similarity's apparent to those who find it. You don't get nothing for nothing: the performance costs, it means you have to be on top of it all the time, and that's exhausting.

Maurice

installed grey airline seats in the Phoenix for a short time, as a pointer to the fact he'd worked for Pan Am, living in pre-revolutionary Tehran to handle incoming tours for Air Express. It was part of the bar's mutable topography; a gallery of signed photos on the walls, the member's lounge in the back, and hireable for private events, just back of Maurice's indomitably personalized domain – his office and high stool facing the entrance steps to look with laser proficiency at each new arrival adjusting to the slightly off-world ambience down there.

Maurice

badged with paste brooches, and invariably wearing one of his ostentatiously attention-grabbing patterned waistcoats maintained a stardust concept of glamour: Maurice's clothes were like his personality dressed. You'd never see him disarranged or dressed down: he was always on as Maurice.

In transit

I write anywhere that's informal, I'd work on poems there, surges of input into a novel, or whatever I happened to be writing that day, but that wasn't conversation with Maurice – it's silent dialogue I do with myself to put my state of reality right. He was actually getting his right in re-angling a red light bulb in its bracket or re-positioning or supplementing a glass for the gin tick.

Maurice

really didn't do outdoors: he slunk. The West End route he crossed daily from Burleigh Mansions to the Phoenix was ten minutes max of daylight, and dead skinny it was a lick, a cigarette cuffed in his hand. I never saw him eat anything, only drink: no foodie gene in his cells, zero understanding of nutrition, fitness or arterial pathways. What Maurice fed on was electrifying interactive nervous energy: the bulleting moment of exchange. He swiped it. Solicitous and generous, he'd heard the lot in his corner and supplied advice if you asked, but was more often general and vicious with repartee.

Maurice

dead, he died reportedly listening to the soundtrack of his favourite *Man of La Mancha*, is now rehabilitated through random memory associations to imagination. I have now to imagine Maurice as he was at the Phoenix, and as he'll never be again: words substituting for his cellular identity: the man who lived for the room he created, members only after 8pm, a cross between a 1950s cocktail lounge and a repurposed Soho dive done with panache, the carefully chosen bar staff intimate, friendly and meticulously alert. There's no waiting time at the counter, drinks are served efficiently fast.

Maurice

led like the letter A for alpha-waves. Whatever he touched was different for him touching it, what was already there went up like stakes on the financial market. He dealt in rhinestones rather than De Beers sparklers, because that was his gestural currency – you made big on affordable tack. You reinvented yourself each moment to stay in it like a nut in nougat. And above all anti-systemic was operative, Maurice ran an extravaganza that was inaccessible to anyone but his clientele.

Maurice

Could never be bought up or out because his one-offish showman-ship wasn't a brand or able to be copied.

Maurice

got there, I mean to the end, as his own creation. What do you do with a deregulated basement, but fixture it with props improvised to attract a type into its déclassé but looks fixated milieu waiting to be drenched in Bassey at 7pm, as Maurice settled to his stool and pushed for refills. Sometimes he was obscured by the fandom of a circle drawn to his insider's track of underground gossip.

Maurice

don't know where you are now or who. I'm in Soho's mauve hydrocarbon blanket, checking out a bookshop on my way to the Phoenix to be submerged in its reassuring cellar. I keep thinking you'll still be there, but you're arguably re-dimensionalized in a different space-time: what do we call the dead, a recombinant virus that writes itself into our nerves, because we can't let them go, unilaterally.

Maurice

they put a silver top hat on your coffin on the shuttle to being incinerated at Golders Green crematorium. I wasn't there, I was writing in my head somewhere, a space in temporal isolation. It rained later that day and I sat listening it out in the Starbucks in Soho's Hollen Street, after the flashy rain came on persistently, and I stayed there because something had ended and I wanted to think only and singularly of

Maurice